From Your Friends at **The MAILBOX®**

P9-BZZ-627

Centered on Learning
WINTER

Over 90 Terrific Seasonal Center Ideas

Table of Contents

More learning center books from *The Mailbox*®

Project Editors: Elizabeth H. Lindsay, Michelle M. Stoffel Menzel, Hope H. Taylor, Jan Trautman
Staff Editors: Cindy K. Daoust, Sherri Lynn Kuntz
Copy Editors: Gina Farago, Karen Brewer Grossman, Karen L. Huffman, Amy Kirtley, Debbie Shoffner
Cover Artists: Nick Greenwood, Kimberly Richard
Art Coordinator: Rebecca Saunders
Artists: Pam Crane, Teresa R. Davidson, Theresa Lewis Goode, Nick Greenwood, Sheila Krill, Clint Moore, Greg D. Rieves, Rebecca Saunders, Barry Slate, Donna K. Teal
Typesetters: Lynette Maxwell, Mark Rainey

President, The Mailbox Book Company™: Joseph C. Bucci
Book Development Managers: Stephen Levy, Elizabeth H. Lindsay, Thad McLaurin, Susan Walker
Book Planning Manager: Chris Poindexter
Curriculum Director: Karen P. Shelton
Traffic Manager: Lisa K. Pitts
Librarian: Dorothy C. McKinney
Editorial and Freelance Management: Karen A. Brudnak
Editorial Training: Irving P. Crump
Editorial Assistants: Terrie Head, Melissa B. Montanez, Hope Rodgers, Jan E. Witcher

©2001 by THE EDUCATION CENTER, INC.
All rights reserved.
ISBN# 1-56234-461-7

Manufactured in the United States
10 9 8 7 6 5 4 3 2 1

About This Book

Focus on fun and learning when you stock your classroom centers with the activities found in *Centered on Learning—Winter*. Just turn the page to find a fresh collection of 15 popular early childhood themes packed with activities for many of your most common learning centers. Each thematic unit includes

▶ Ideas and skills that are easily scanned, so you can choose the centers you need based on your students' needs

▶ All-new center ideas that reinforce curriculum concepts and skills

▶ Independent and small-group learning activities

▶ Ideas to help coordinate your centers with your current topics of study

Centered on Learning—Winter helps make planning simple, too! Since many of the units correspond to themes you already teach, all you need to do is scan the skills in each unit and then make your center selections. So use *Centered on Learning—Winter* to make the most of your valuable time and your classroom learning center opportunities!

Gingerbread Junction

Goodness gracious—it's gingerbread time! Serve up these sweet centers for lots of learning fun.

by Sherri Lynn Kuntz

Literacy Center

▶ story retelling
▶ experience with text
▶ expressive language skills

Gingerbread Storytelling

Your students will run, run, run as fast as they can to this story retelling center! In advance, spread a coat of glue all over the bowl of a plastic spoon; then sprinkle ginger and cinnamon on it. When the glue is dry, put the spoon in a basket along with a small bowl, a gingerbread man cookie cutter, artificial greenery, and wooden blocks. Cover a table with a decorative tablecloth and place the filled basket and a cookie sheet under the table. After sharing your favorite versions of *The Gingerbread Man*, display the books on the table. Invite students to explore the book selections and use the props to retell the story.

Math Center

▶ reproducing shapes
▶ spatial awareness
▶ fine-motor skills

Sh-Sh-Shape It!

Candies that are typically used to decorate gingerbread cookies and cottages make great manipulatives for little hands! In advance, duplicate the shape cards (page 7) onto construction paper. Color, cut out, and laminate the cards. Store the cards in a recipe box. Place the recipe box in a center along with a class supply of napkins and an assortment of small candies, such as gumdrops, red hots, and peppermint discs. When a child visits the center, have her take a napkin to use as her workspace. Then ask her to choose a shape card from the box. Encourage her to use the candies to reproduce that shape on her napkin. Then have her clear off her napkin and choose another shape card. Invite her to repeat the activity until she has made each shape. Look! A gumdrop triangle!

The Cookie Jar

This particular cookie jar provides fine-motor practice with the scent of ginger and a side order of math skills, too! In advance, fill a plastic jar with large gingersnaps. Place the jar in a center along with a pair of tongs, a medium-sized cookie sheet, a pencil, and scrap paper. Invite each child to estimate the number of cookies it will take to cover the sheet. After he writes down his guess, have him use the tongs to place the cookies side by side on the sheet. When the cookie sheet is covered, have the child count the number of gingersnaps used and compare it to his guess.

Cottage Creations

Spice up your sensory center with this cottage-making idea! In advance, prepare a batch of Gingerbread Play Dough. Put the play dough in your sensory center along with a rolling pin, cookie cutters, and small assorted candies or cake decorations. When a child visits the center, encourage him to use the supplies to make a pretend gingerbread cottage. (Although this dough smells mighty nice, it's just for hands-on fun!)

Sensory Center

creative ◄
expression
tactile ◄
experience
spatial awareness ◄

Gingerbread Play Dough

Ingredients:
1¹/₂ c. all-purpose flour
1 c. salt
1 tbsp. powdered alum
1 tbsp. vegetable oil
1 c. boiling water
brown paste food coloring
1 tbsp. pumpkin pie spice

Directions:
In a large bowl, combine the flour, salt, and alum. Add the oil and boiling water; then stir until well blended. Add the spice and coloring; then knead the dough until it is smooth. Store the dough in an airtight container.

Home, *Sweet* Home

Dramatic-Play Center

▶ *creative thinking*
▶ *role-playing*
▶ *verbal skills*

Tempt your students' imaginations with this dramatic-play center. In advance, make a cottage by using a craft knife to cut a door and two window openings in a large brown appliance box. Next, refer to the ideas below to make pretend candies. Attach a Velcro® dot to the back of each candy piece. Then attach the corresponding Velcro dots to the cottage. Arrange the cottage and candies in a center along with wooden blocks. When students visit the center, invite them to decorate the cottage and use the blocks to make a gingerbread path. Knock, knock!

Gumdrop
Paint a Styrofoam® ball half with a mixture of one part Elmer's® glue and two parts tempera paint. Sprinkle clear glitter on top of the paint; then set it aside to dry.

Lollipop
Tape a large craft stick to the flat side of a plastic lid. On the opposite side, use a permanent marker to make designs.

Peppermint Stick
Tape the ends of two lengths of red yarn to the top inside of a white cardboard tube. Wrap the yarn around the tube to resemble stripes. Then tape the other ends to the bottom inside of the tube. (Striped straws can also be used to resemble smaller peppermint sticks.)

Peppermint Disc
Use a marker to draw swirls on any size Styrofoam® ball. Wrap the ball with clear plastic wrap; then tie each end with a length of yarn.

Ginger Candy

Cooking Center

▶ *following directions*
▶ *fine-motor skills*
▶ *sensory experience*

This gingery treat is sure to stir up your youngsters' senses! In advance, mix up a batch of candy dough (see the recipe below). Sandwich the dough between two sheets of waxed paper; then place it in your cooking center. Also provide a supply of gumdrops, napkins, and a plastic knife. Invite each center visitor to knead the dough through the waxed paper. Then have her lift the top layer of waxed paper and cut off a small portion of dough (about the size of a quarter). After she rolls her dough into a ball, have her press a gumdrop into the center. Ready to eat!

Ingredients:
one 3-oz. package of cream cheese, softened
3 c. powdered sugar
1 tbsp. cinnamon
1/2 tsp. ground ginger

Directions:
1. Mix the cream cheese, cinnamon, and ground ginger in a bowl. Add a cup of powdered sugar at a time and mix until a dough forms.
2. Knead the dough thoroughly, adding extra powdered sugar if the dough becomes sticky.

Shapin' Up!

Circles and triangles and squares—oh my!
Give these shapely centers a try!

by Dayle Timmons

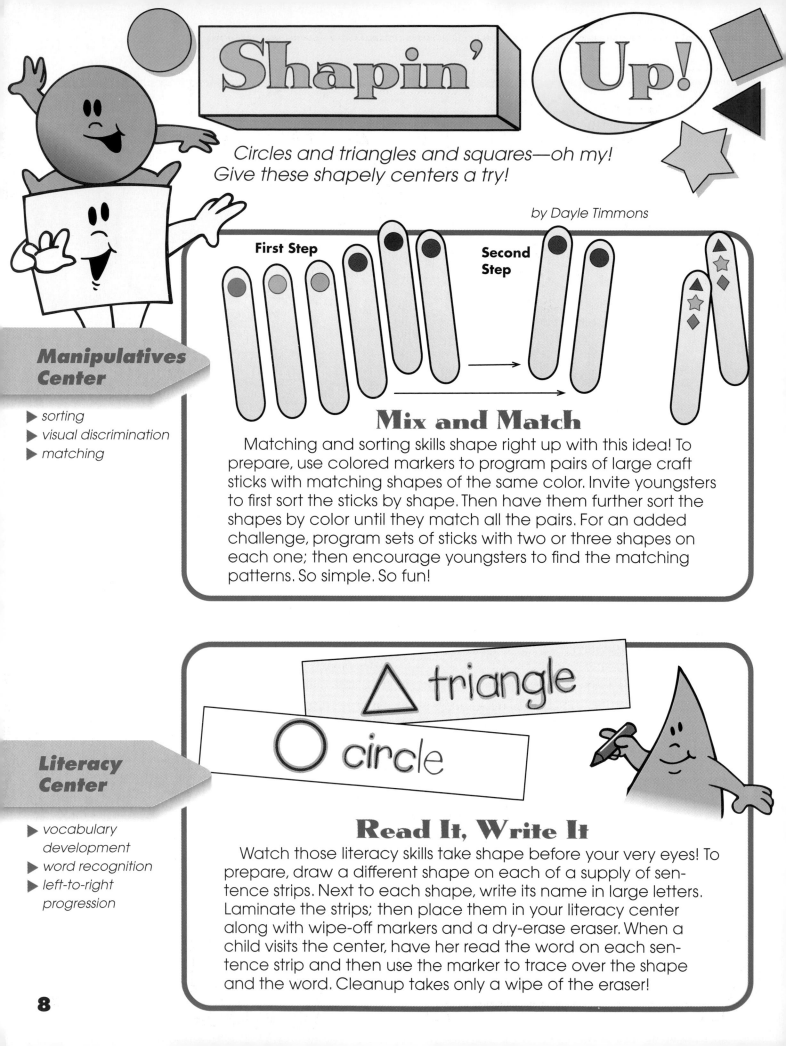

Manipulatives Center

▶ sorting
▶ visual discrimination
▶ matching

First Step

Second Step

Mix and Match

Matching and sorting skills shape right up with this idea! To prepare, use colored markers to program pairs of large craft sticks with matching shapes of the same color. Invite youngsters to first sort the sticks by shape. Then have them further sort the shapes by color until they match all the pairs. For an added challenge, program sets of sticks with two or three shapes on each one; then encourage youngsters to find the matching patterns. So simple. So fun!

Literacy Center

▶ vocabulary development
▶ word recognition
▶ left-to-right progression

△ triangle

○ circle

Read It, Write It

Watch those literacy skills take shape before your very eyes! To prepare, draw a different shape on each of a supply of sentence strips. Next to each shape, write its name in large letters. Laminate the strips; then place them in your literacy center along with wipe-off markers and a dry-erase eraser. When a child visits the center, have her read the word on each sentence strip and then use the marker to trace over the shape and the word. Cleanup takes only a wipe of the eraser!

Shape Bags

The preparation for *this* discovery center goes to your students! Give each child a paper lunch bag and ask him to draw a shape on one panel. Then have him take the bag home and find something that is the same shape. As the shape bags come back to school, have each child place his object in your discovery center. Then encourage youngsters to take a closer look to see how many shapes they can discover. Hey—a rectangle scarf!

Water Wonders

Shapes in the water table? Sure! Why not? To prepare, cut out a variety of shapes from craft foam. Use a permanent marker to trace each shape onto a foam tray. Scatter the shapes in the water and stack the programmed trays nearby. When a child visits this center, have her float the trays on the water. Then encourage her to search the water to find a shape to match each corresponding outline on the trays.

Sensory
Center

creative ◄
exploration
sorting ◄
counting ◄

Magic Act

You won't need magic words to see the trick at this center! Use chalk to draw shapes near the bottom of your chalkboard. (If you have only individual lap chalkboards, draw shapes on each one of those instead.) Provide large paintbrushes (or small paintbrushes for lap boards) and water. Invite children to use the brushes and water to paint over the shapes. Surprise! The shapes disappear!

Block Shapes

Continue to work with shapes in your block center! On the floor of your block area, use colored tape to create large outlines of different shapes. For this activity, have a child select a type of block to arrange along the outline of a shape. How many blocks will it take to cover the tape? Will there be enough blocks? What will she do if she runs out of blocks? What a fun way to review shapes and build problem-solving skills!

Sing a Song of Shapes

Is that the sound of music you hear? Absolutely! For each shape that you're studying, cut out two or three large construction paper samples; then laminate them. Store the shapes in a string-tie envelope. Then make a tape recording of the song below, substituting a different shape each time you repeat the verse. Place the shapes in a center along with the tape and a tape player. Invite one to three children at a time to listen to the song and manipulate the shape cutouts according to the song. Tune in to shapes!

If You Have a Circle
(sung to the tune of "Did You Ever See a Lassie?")

Oh, if you have a (circle), a (circle), a (circle),
Oh, if you have a (circle), then hold it up high!
Wave it this way and that way,
Then that way and this way.
Oh, if you have a (circle), then hold it up high!

Music and Movement Center

listening skills ◄
following directions ◄
shape recognition ◄

The Shape of Art

Shapes galore create art and more! Cut a supply of geometric shapes from light-colored construction paper. Then put the shapes in a center along with crayons, markers, glue, art paper, and assorted art supplies. Have each youngster choose one or more shapes to transform into a picture. Will the circle become a smiley face? A snowball? A big, bright sun? Just shape it up to see!

Art Center

shape ◄
discrimination
creative ◄
expression
spatial awareness ◄

Bakery Bonanza

Stir up a fresh batch of unique activities with these bakery centers!

by Mackie Rhodes

Reading Recipes

Serve up reading and prereading success with this simple recipe! In advance, collect a supply of empty cake-mix boxes that have easy-to-read picture recipes. Also gather items to correspond with the utensils and ingredients pictured, such as measuring cups and spoons, plastic eggs, and an empty oil bottle. Place the items in a center. Next, invite a child to select a box and find the directions. Have him "read" the recipe and then find the utensils and ingredients corresponding to the illustrated directions. Once he's gathered all of the utensils and ingredients, he's ready to start pretend cooking! Now that's a recipe for prereading success!

Literacy Center

▶ left-to-right progression
▶ following directions
▶ experience with print

Bakery Balance

Adding flour to a balance scale will give your youngsters just what they need to make measurement discoveries. Simply stock these two items in your discovery center along with small margarine tubs and measuring spoons. When a child visits this center, have her place a tub on each tray of a balance scale and then scoop spoonfuls of flour into each tub until the scale balances. Hey, little bakers, measuring flour is fun!

Discovery Center

▶ exploration
▶ observation
▶ problem solving

Pretzels to Go

Order up a batch of sorting and counting skills when you transform your math center into a pretzel shop. To prepare, gather a supply of resealable plastic bags and pretzels in various shapes, such as sticks, twists, and fish. Draw a pretzel shape on each bag; then label the bag with a numeral from 1 to 10. Mix all the pretzels in a large bowl; then arrange all the supplies mentioned in a center along with an apron and a chef's hat. Have a student baker don the apron and hat while a customer selects a few labeled pretzel bags. The customer gives the bags to the baker, who then fills each bag with the corresponding number of pretzels with the matching shape. The baker returns the bag to the customer, who then checks it for accuracy. Here you are, sir—eight pretzel sticks to go!

The Pretzel Shop

Math Center

sorting ◄
numeral ◄
recognition
counting ◄

Cupcake Cuties

Delight students with cute characters fashioned after a favorite bakery treat—the cupcake! In advance, stock a center with the materials listed below. Encourage each child to use the supplies to create a cupcake character. (If desired, refer to the directions below.) Use the finished projects to adorn your classroom bakery display. Ahhh, what a cutie!

Materials needed for each child:
1 white construction paper copy of the cupcake (page 15)
assorted construction paper scraps
crayons
glue
scissors
a variety of cake-decorating supplies

Art Center

fine-motor skills ◄
creative ◄
expression
tactile experience ◄

Directions:
1. Cut out the cupcake pattern and color it as desired.
2. Cut out construction paper arms and legs; then glue them to the back of the cupcake.
3. To add facial features, glue on your choice of cake-decorating supplies.

▶ *tactile experience*
▶ *socialization*
▶ *creative play*

It's Hand Mixed!

Little fingers will eagerly explore this sweet-smelling mixture! Simply add one 26-ounce carton of salt and one box of chocolate cake mix to each five-pound bag of flour you pour into the sensory tub. Also stock the center with aprons, flour sifters, mixing bowls, wooden spoons, and cake pans. Then invite your students to stir, scoop, and sift to their hearts' content. If you don't have a sink nearby, provide a tub of water and paper towels. (Save the mixture to use in "Cake-Mix Play Dough.")

▶ *fine-motor skills*
▶ *sensory experience*

Cake-Mix Play Dough

"Knead" a new twist in your fine-motor center? Then mixing up this batch of unique dough is the answer! Make a batch of cake-mix play dough using the recipe below. Place the dough in a center along with rolling pins, muffin tins, cupcake liners, and an assortment of cookie cutters. Then invite youngsters' imaginations to take over. Yeah! We're rollin' that dough!

Cake-Mix Play Dough
3 c. mix from "It's Hand Mixed!" (above)
2 tsp. cooking oil
$3/4$ c. water

In a medium bowl, stir together all the ingredients until a stiff dough forms. Store the dough in an airtight container.

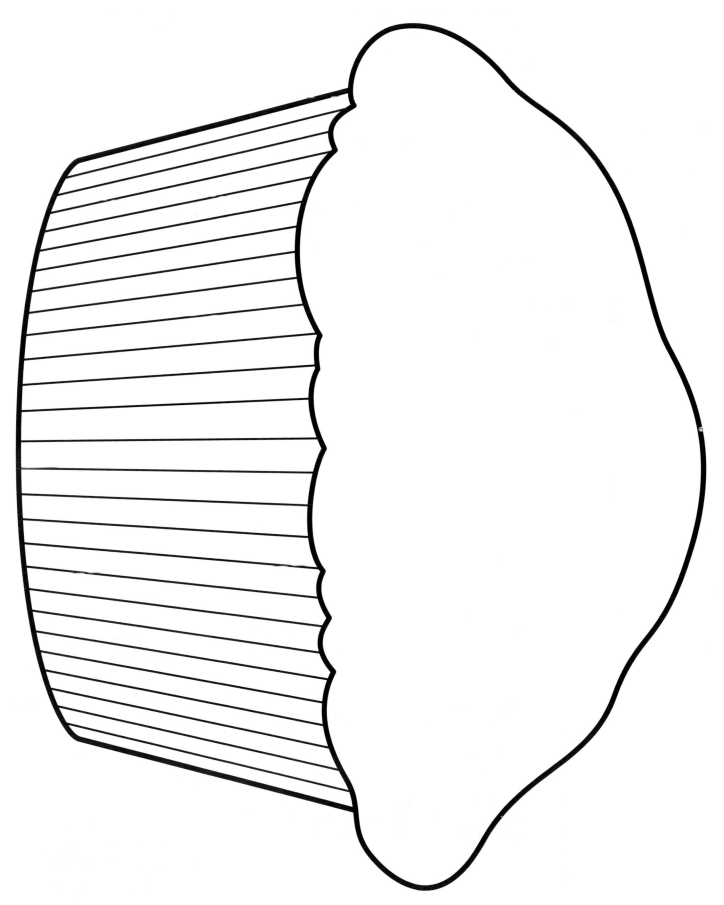

Penguin Pals

Pal up with penguins for lots of playful learning at these curriculum-friendly centers.

by Mackie Rhodes

Math Center

▶ *size discrimination*
▶ *numeral sequencing*

Everybody, Line Up!

Practice size seriation with these penguin pals. First, color and cut out a copy of the penguin family on page 19. Glue each penguin to a different foam cup as shown. Using a permanent marker, label the back rim of each cup with a numeral from 1 to 5 to show the size order of the penguins *from smallest to largest*. To do this activity, ask a child to arrange the penguins by size in a side-by-side line. To check her work, have the child check (or ask you to check) the numeral sequence on the cups. For an added challenge, have a child stack the cups by penguin size, beginning with the *largest* penguin on the bottom.

Literacy Center

▶ *color words*
▶ *experience with print*

Fancy Penguins

Plenty of color-word practice awaits your youngsters when they dress these penguins in style! For each color that you'd like to include, copy the penguin and bow tie patterns (page 19) on white construction paper. Write a different color word on the belly of each penguin and color a bow tie to match. Color and cut out the penguins; then laminate all the patterns.

To do this activity, have a child match each bow tie to the penguin with the corresponding color word. All dressed up!

Ready, Set, Slide!

Slip and slide into measurement skills with these playful penguins! To make one penguin, copy the smallest pattern from the penguin family on page 19. Then fill an empty black film canister with sand and snap on the lid. Next, glue the penguin pattern to the canister. Place all the penguins in an uncarpeted area of your room, along with a supply of unlined index cards (to resemble icebergs). Use masking tape to designate a starting line. When a child visits this center, have her kneel at the starting line and slide a penguin across the floor. Then ask her to use the icebergs to measure the distance. How many icebergs? Invite the child to repeat the penguin slide again and compare the distances. Whee!

Discovery Center

measurement ◄
skills
counting ◄

Swim, Penguins, Swim!

Dive right in and experience this very unique version of surf and sea. To prepare, use a fine-tip permanent marker to draw a simple penguin on each of a supply of large lima beans. Fill a sensory tub with rice (tinted blue if you like!); then bury the penguins in it. When a child visits the center, have him comb through the "waters" with his hands to catch the swimming penguins. If desired, post a specified number of penguins to find each day and challenge students to find exactly that many. Swim, penguins, swim!

Sensory Center

tactile ◄
discrimination
visual ◄
discrimination
fine-motor skills ◄

Perky Little Penguins

These magnets make great math manipulatives for school or adorable refrigerator pals for home. To prepare, make tracers by cutting out tagboard copies of the penguin body on page 19. Place these tracers in a center along with wooden craft spoons, black craft foam, orange construction paper scraps, wiggle eyes, craft glue, and blue pens. To make a penguin, use the pen to trace the penguin body pattern onto the black craft foam; then cut it out. (For younger children, provide precut foam shapes.) Glue a craft spoon onto the black cutout to resemble the penguin's head and body. Then glue on wiggle eyes and an orange construction paper beak and feet. To complete the penguin, attach a strip of magnetic tape to the back. Hello, little pal!

Penguin Playground

Invite little ones to use their imaginations to create a pretend romp for penguins. Gather miscellaneous white packaging items such as Styrofoam® pieces and peanuts. In preparation, make several penguins as described in "Ready, Set, Slide!" on page 17. Place the penguins and white supplies in your block center. Then invite children to invent a playground for penguins. Before you know it, you'll have banks, icebergs, and even sloping hills. Penguins, get ready to waddle, slide, dive, and glide!

penguin family
Use with "Everybody, Line Up!" on page 16 and use the
smallest penguin with "Ready, Set, Slide!" on page 17.

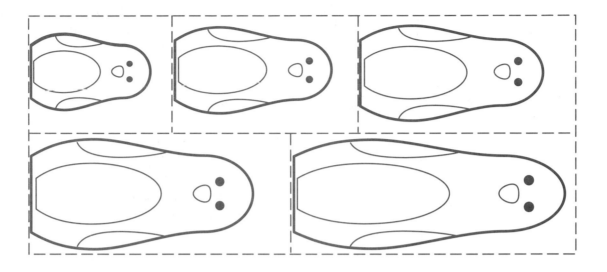

bow tie and penguin
Use with "Fancy Penguins" on page 16.

penguin body
Use with "Perky Little Penguins" on page 18.

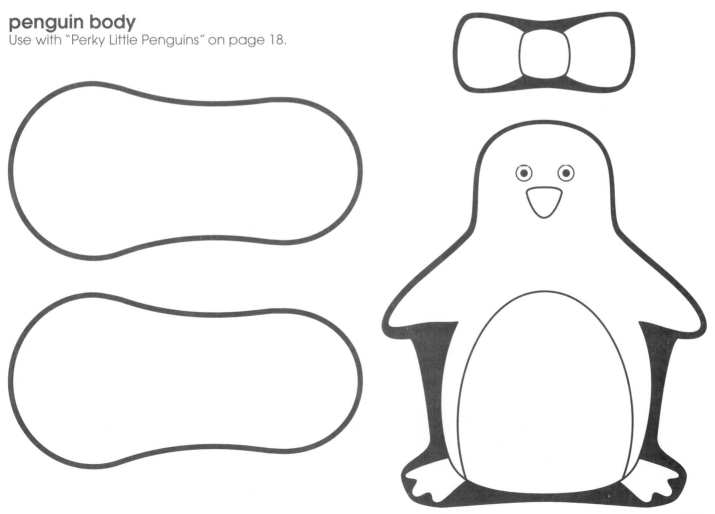

Snow Daze

Bundle up for lots of wintry learning with these snow-packed ideas!

by Roxanne LaBell Dearman

Math Center

▶ *reproducing shapes*
▶ *spatial awareness*

Snowball Shapes

Add a flurry of excitement to your math center using shape mats and fluffy little snowballs. To make the mats, you'll need several 9" x 12" sheets of blue construction paper. Draw a different shape on each mat; then laminate the mats. Place them in a center along with a pile of cotton balls (to represent snowballs). When a child visits the center, have him select a mat and then arrange the snowballs to create the matching shape on the mat. Encourage him to select additional mats to create a blizzard of snowy shapes!

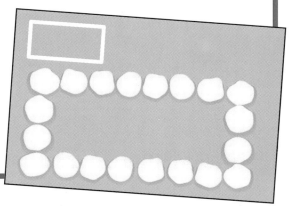

Discovery Center

▶ *observation skills*
▶ *predictions*
▶ *visual discrimination*

The Facts of Ice

Invite your little ones to explore the facts of ice with this freeze-and-melt center. Half-fill clear plastic bottles with water and freeze them. Next, add an object, such as a toy car or a teddy bear counter to each bottle. Top off each bottle with water, leaving a little air space at the top; then refreeze. Place the bottles at a center along with a couple tubs of water. Encourage students to visit this center early in the day to explore and make predictions. Later in the day, invite children to check on the bottles to explore and discover some more!

Think Snow

Literacy Center

creative writing ◄
writing skills ◄

What Do You Do When It Starts to Snow?

By Ms. Brown's Class

I go slede with my dad Casey

After sharing a snowy tale, such as *When It Starts to Snow* by Phillis Gershator, invite each child to visit the literacy center to create a page for a snowy class booklet. Provide a supply of round coffee filters and crayons. When a child visits this center, ask her to draw a picture on a coffee filter to show what she does (or would like to do) when it snows. Next, have her write or dictate about her illustration. When each child has completed a page, bind all the pages behind a coffee-filter title page. Invite each child to share her page during a group time. Let it snow!

Snowflake Flurry

Sensory Center

visual discrimination ◄
fine-motor skills ◄

Shovel up a pile of visual discrimination skills with this snowflake exploration activity. To begin, cut out several pairs of matching snowflakes from white craft foam. Bury the snowflakes in a sensory tub filled with rice. Then add a couple of sand shovels. As children shovel the snow, encourage them to find matching pairs of snowflakes. Shovels ready? This forecast calls for snowflake flurries!

Making Tracks

Art Center

▶ *creative expression*
▶ *spatial awareness*
▶ *fine-motor skills*

Looking for inspiration for wintertime art? *The Snowy Day* by Ezra Jack Keats delivers! In advance, stock your art center with white art paper, white paint tinted to a very light shade of blue, and craft sponges cut in the shape of footprints. After sharing the story, open your art center for snowy-day creativity! When a child visits the center, have him use the footprint-shaped sponges and paint to make footprints on a sheet of art paper. (If desired, encourage children to make prints with other story-inspired objects, such as small twigs.) When the paint is dry, help each child mount his painting on a colorful sheet of construction paper.

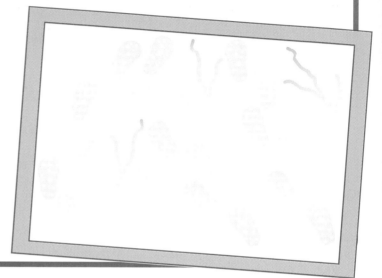

Snowy Snack

Cooking Center

▶ *left-to-right progression*
▶ *following directions*
▶ *fine-motor skills*

Your little ones will be proud to independently prepare their own snowy snacks. In advance, copy, color, and cut out the recipe cards on page 23. Display the cards in your cooking area. Review the recipe with your class; then invite each child to visit the center and make his own snowy snack.

Snowy Snack

Ingredients per child:
$1/4$ c. Frosted Cheerios®
$1/4$ c. mini marshmallows
1 tbsp. shredded coconut

Utensils and supplies:
one 4-c. coffee filter per child
one 20-oz. plastic jar with lid

Teacher preparation:
Arrange the ingredients and utensils for easy student access.

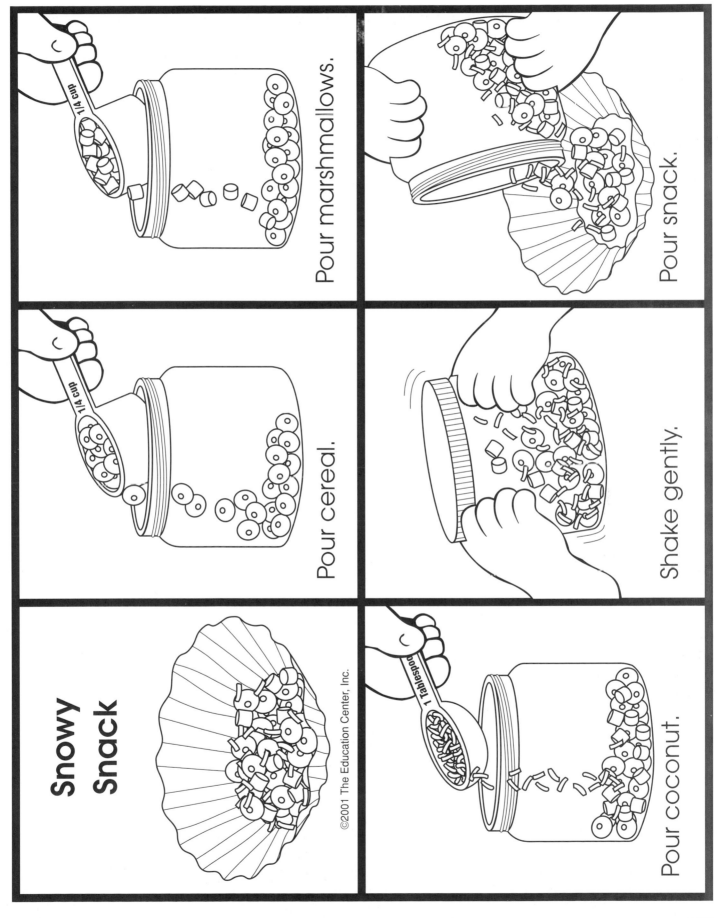

Pour marshmallows.

Pour snack.

Pour cereal.

Shake gently.

Snowy Snack

©2001 The Education Center, Inc.

Pour coconut.

Marvelous Mittens

Want to keep your youngsters' skills warmed up? Create the perfect learning climate with these mitten-inspired centers!

by Audrey McNeill

Literacy Center

▶ name recognition
▶ experience with print

Mitten Match

Whose mittens are these? Your youngsters will find out with this reading activity. In advance, duplicate the pair of mittens on page 27 onto various colors of construction paper to make a class supply. For each child, cut out a pair of same-colored mittens. Program one mitten with the child's name; then glue that child's photo on the matching mitten. Laminate all the cutouts; then place them in a center. When a child visits this center, have him read the name on a mitten and then pair it with the corresponding photo on another mitten. For older children, program mittens with first and last names. Hey, Zachary! I found your mittens!

Which Is Warmer?

In your discovery center, provide several different types of mittens, including a waterproof pair. Place a bucket of snow (or ice cubes) in the center; then invite youngsters to dig in! Instruct each child to explore the snow using the different types of mittens and discuss her discoveries. It won't take long to discover that dry mittens are warm mittens!

Discovery Center

▶ sensory experience
▶ making comparisons
▶ drawing conclusions

24

Lacing Mittens

Give little hands big fine-motor practice with these sturdy lacing mittens. To make them, use a permanent marker to trace the outline of the mitten patterns (page 27) onto colorful plastic placemats and then cut them out. Hole-punch around the perimeter of each mitten. Place the mittens in a center along with plastic needles and a supply of brightly colored laces. (For younger children, thread each needle; then tie the end of the yarn around one of the holes at the bottom of a mitten cutout.) Invite youngsters to lace around the mittens.

Motor Center

fine-motor skills ◄
patterning ◄

Mittens and More

If your children enjoy activities using the popular "feely box" idea, try this sensory table twist. In advance, gather several different pairs of mittens and put them in a pillowcase. Invite a child to reach inside the pillowcase and pull out one mitten. Then have him reach in the pillowcase again and try to find that mitten's match without looking. Encourage the child to repeat the activity until all the mittens have been matched.

Sensory Center

sorting ◄
tactile ◄
discrimination

▶ fine-motor skills
▶ sorting

Mitten Clip

The mitten laundry is now open! Stock a laundry basket with a variety of mittens. Place the laundry basket in your dramatic-play area along with a supply of clothespins. Then make a clothesline by stringing a length of rope between two chairs. When a child visits this center, have him clip the mittens onto the clothesline. Encourage him to be creative as he thinks of different ways to sort and arrange the mittens.

▶ visual
  discrimination
▶ patterning

Mitten Patterns

These festive mittens are a perfect match for a patterning center! Make mitten tracers from the patterns on page 27. Trace a large supply of mitten shapes onto different types of craft paper; then cut them out. Laminate all the cutouts; then place them in your math center. Have youngsters who visit the center use the mittens to make patterns.

Mitten Patterns

Use with "Mitten Match" on page 24, "Lacing Mittens" on page 25,
and "Mitten Patterns" on page 26.

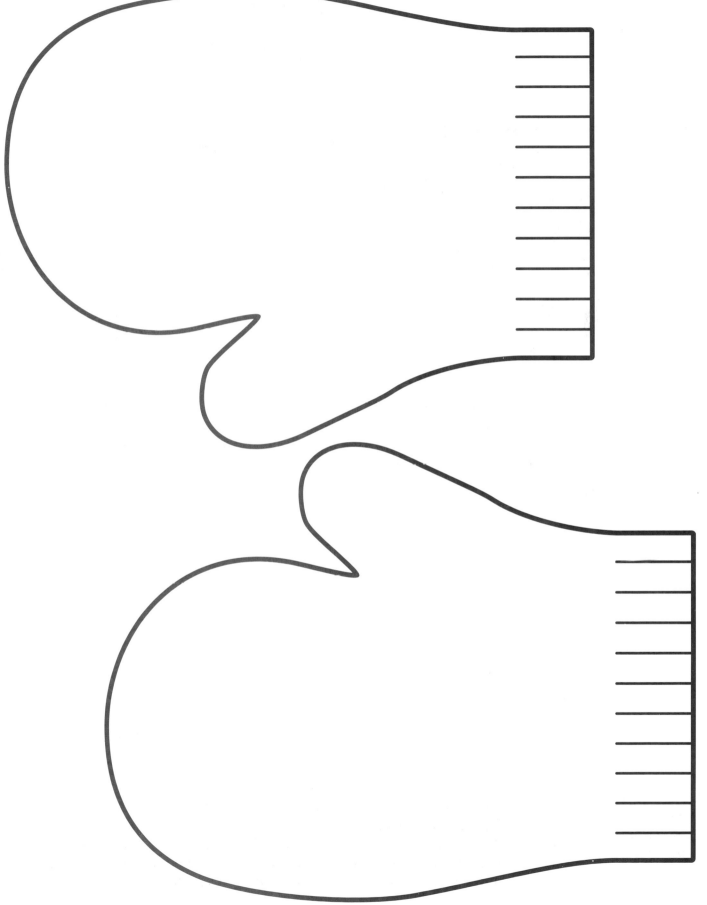

27

Forever Evergreens!

Spruce up your centers with these fun tree-related activities!

by Kim Love

Literacy Center

▶ letter recognition
▶ sequencing letters
▶ left-to-right progression

An Alphabet Forest

Trim up those alphabet skills with an interactive forest! In advance, paint 26 cone-shaped paper cups green. When the paint is dry, label each cup (tree) with a different letter of the alphabet. For this activity, have a child arrange the trees in alphabetical order. To top it off, invite the child to sing the alphabet song and tap each tree as she sings the corresponding letter.

Discovery Center

▶ observation skills
▶ sensory experience

Exploring Evergreens

The attributes of evergreens take root in this discovery center! In advance, send a copy of the parent note (page 31) home with each child. When the evergreen clippings and pinecones arrive at school, arrange them in your discovery center along with some paper, pencils, crayons, and magnifying lenses. Invite your students to visit the center to explore, examine, sort, and classify. Encourage children to write about and illustrate their discoveries.

The Great Indoor Woodland

Pining for an exciting twist to add to your sensory center? Here it is! Spread a layer of clean pine or cedar shavings in your sensory table. Add dump trucks and other toys that are just right for hauling, measuring, and pouring. As children play, encourage them to work with the concepts of *full, empty, more,* and *less.* What a great day for woodland play!

Razzle-Dazzle Evergreens

Evergreen paintbrushes make this seasonal art idea unique! To make a paintbrush, wrap a paper towel around the end of an evergreen branch. Then secure the paper towel with masking tape. Supply your art area with several evergreen paintbrushes, green paint, white art paper, and glitter. Have each center visitor use the evergreen paintbrushes to paint a picture. While the paint is still wet, invite the child to sprinkle glitter on his work. When the paint is dry, mount each picture on a colorful sheet of construction paper. Then arrange all the pictures on a bulletin board to create a dazzling evergreen display!

Art
Center

creative expression ◄
exploring texture ◄
fine-motor skills ◄

29

Dancing Trees

Evergreen costumes provide the perfect inspiration for little dancers! To make one branch, cut a slit along the length of a cardboard tube. Then fringe-cut along one side of a strip of green construction paper. Glue the fringed paper along the length of the tube. Place several (an even number) of these branch costumes in your music center. Also provide a selection of wintry music. When children visit this center, invite them to wear the branches on their arms, turn on the music, and move as the music inspires them. See the forest of dancing trees!

Teeny, Tiny Trees

With this science center activity, little green trees will be sprouting up all over your classroom! In advance, soak a class supply of pinecones in water overnight. Put the pinecones in your science center along with a tub of potting soil, a shallow tub of grass seed, a water-filled spray bottle, and a class supply of foam bowls. When a child visits the center, have her roll a pinecone in the potting soil and then lightly mist it with water. Next, have her roll the soil-covered pinecone in the grass seed. Instruct the child to set the seed-covered pinecone in a bowl and lightly mist it again. Encourage the child to predict what will happen to her pinecone. Then have each child place her project near a sunny window, periodically misting it with water and observing what happens over several days. Watch for little green surprises!

Dear Parent,

Our class is going to study evergreens. Please help your child pick out several evergreen branch clippings and/or pinecones. Then send your collection to school with your child on

_____.

Thanks for your support!

©2001 The Education Center, Inc. • *Centered on Learning* • *Winter* • TEC3518

Dear Parent,

Our class is going to study evergreens. Please help your child pick out several evergreen branch clippings and/or pinecones. Then send your collection to school with your child on

_____.

Thanks for your support!

©2001 The Education Center, Inc. • *Centered on Learning* • *Winter* • TEC3518

TERRIFIC TEETH

Use these dental-health centers to brush up on cross-curricular skills!

by Mackie Rhodes

Toothy Grins

Math Center

▶ counting
▶ number and/or number-word recognition
▶ fine-motor skills

This center activity will bring miles of tooth-bearing smiles. For each number that you'd like to include in this center, duplicate the mouth pattern (page 35) on red construction paper. Cut out each pattern; then mount it on a poster board card. Program each card with a numeral or number word; then laminate the cards. Store all the cards and a bag of miniature marshmallows (or small dried lima beans) in a large resealable bag. For this activity, a child arranges all the mouth cards on a flat surface. Then he places the appropriate number of marshmallow (or lima bean) teeth inside each mouth. Grin and count it!

Pearly Whites

Art Center

▶ creative expression
▶ fine-motor skills

These pearly whites have personality! For each child, enlarge and copy a tooth pattern (page 35) on white construction paper. Place the patterns in a center along with crayons, markers, scissors, glue, craft sticks, and various art supplies. When a child visits this center, invite her to transform a tooth cutout into a tooth puppet by adding clothing, hair, and facial features. Then have her glue a craft stick to the back of her puppet. During a group time, have each child use her puppet as she sings the song in the music and movement center (page 34).

Toothpaste Box Puzzles

Kids love puzzles! And they'll love the unique twist of using recycled toothpaste boxes. In advance, ask parents to send in empty toothpaste boxes in a variety of brands. To make one puzzle, use a craft knife to puzzle-cut the box into three sections. Tape the ends with clear tape; then tape crumpled paper inside each piece so that the box retains its three-dimensional shape. Place all the pieces in a basket In your center. For this activity, encourage a child to find three puzzle pieces that go together. Then have her arrange the pieces so that they reveal a kind of toothpaste. Look! It's Sparkle!

I'm in Advertising Now!

Smile and put your best jingle forward! Stock a center with a supply of white construction paper, crayons, markers, scissors, old magazines, and glue. For this activity, ask each child to think of a new kind of toothpaste. Encourage her to design an ad for her original product by using the supplies to illustrate and write about it. During a group time, have each child share her ad with the class. Afterward, bind all the pages together to make a class book of newly invented toothpastes.

Dental Discoveries

Discovery Center

▶ observation skills
▶ counting
▶ recording information

To set up this center, position a mirror at child height. Also provide a supply of paper, crayons, and pencils. Before opening this center, prompt children with questions such as the following: What color are your teeth? How many teeth do you have? Are any of your teeth missing or loose? What keeps your teeth in your mouth? Instruct each child to wash his hands before taking a turn in the center. Then have him take a peek in the mirror at his own teeth to see what he can find out! Encourage children to write about and illustrate their discoveries.

Brushing Melody

Music and Movement Center

▶ rhythm
▶ oral language
▶ creative thinking

Invite your students to use the puppets they have made in the art center (page 32) as they sing the song below. These pearly whites have something to sing about!

Take Care of Us!
(sung to the tune of "Row, Row, Row Your Boat")

Brush, brush, brush us, please.
Brush us every day.
Brush, brush, brush us, please,
To fight that tooth decay!

Rinse, rinse, rinse us, please.
Rinse us every day.
Rinse, rinse, rinse us, please,
To fight that tooth decay!

Eat, eat, eat good foods
To keep us mighty strong.
Eat, eat, eat good foods,
And we'll last very long!

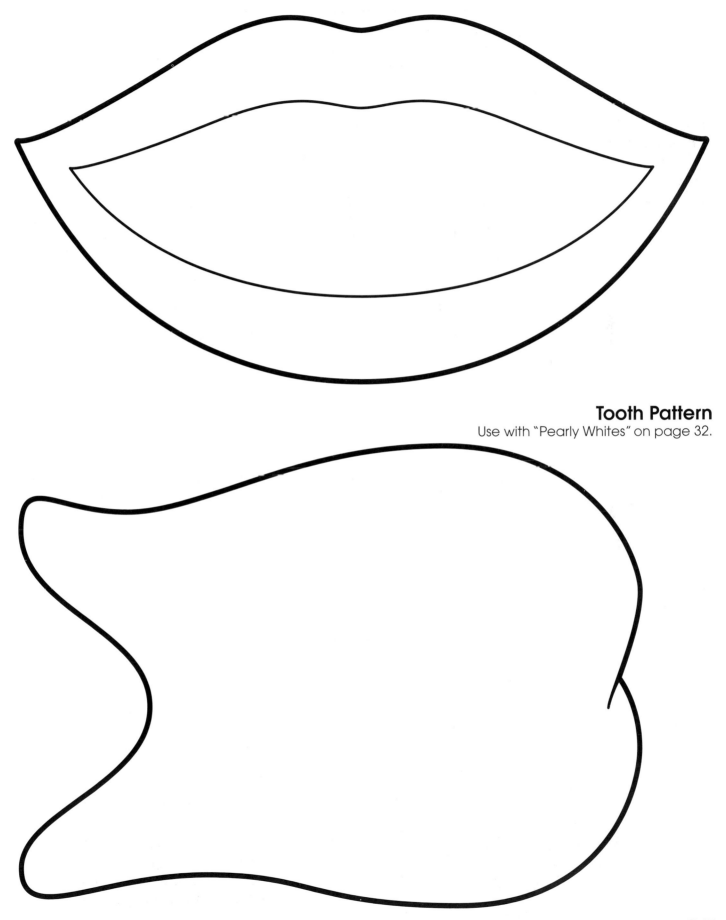

Mouth Pattern
Use with "Toothy Grins" on page 32.

Tooth Pattern
Use with "Pearly Whites" on page 32.

SWEET HEARTS

Sweeten youngsters' appetite for learning with these heart-related center ideas!

by Sandra Faulkner

Counting Hearts

Math Center

▶ counting
▶ measurement
▶ estimation

Math skills beat right along with this "heart-y" center idea. To prepare, stock a center with a few empty heart-shaped boxes, small gift boxes, and a bowl of candy conversation hearts. Encourage children to create different ways to arrange the candies inside the boxes. How many candies does it take to go *around* the shape of each box? To go *across* each box? To divide each box right down the middle? If desired, keep an unhandled batch of conversation hearts available to reward a job well done!

Hearts So Full

Sensory Center

▶ fine-motor skills
▶ tactile experience
▶ observation skills

Here's an idea that's soaked with learning opportunities! In advance, cut out a supply of heart shapes from a variety of craft sponges. Sprinkle heart-shaped confetti in your water table and, if desired, use red food coloring to tint the water. Place the dry sponges near the water along with some bowls and cups. As little ones visit this center, invite them to observe what happens when they dunk the sponges in the water. Also prompt children to see how much water they can squeeze out of the water-soaked sponges.

Friendship Bracelets

This lovely piece of jewelry might look like a simple bracelet, but you'll know it's a creative tool for reinforcing friendships and fine-motor skills. Provide a supply of pipe cleaners along with a large supply of craft beads. When a child visits this center, have him choose a pipe cleaner and then string on his selection of beads in the pattern of his choice. Have him twist the ends together to make a bracelet sized to slip over his hand. When everyone has made a bracelet, encourage each child to trade bracelets with a classmate. From my heart to yours!

Motor Center

fine-motor skills ◄
patterning ◄
socialization ◄

Disappearing Hearts

What happens to candy hearts when they are immersed in warm water? How about ice water? Or just left out in the air? Invite your youngsters to investigate and find out for themselves! Stock the center with a supply of candy conversation hearts, clear plastic cups, craft sticks (for stirring), and a bowl of ice. Before opening this center, prompt students to make predictions by asking the questions mentioned above. Next, have a child put an ice cube in a cup. Then have her fill the cup with cold water and fill another cup with warm water. Encourage children to use the supplies to find out what happens to candy hearts left in the different places. Any ideas *why*?

Discovery Center

observation ◄
prediction ◄
experimentation ◄

Here's a Heart!

Your students will definitely deliver when it comes to passing along these heartfelt sentiments. In advance, stock a center with a variety of valentines or construction paper heart cutouts. Also provide markers, stickers, envelopes, a class list, and a mailbox (or decorated box). Encourage children visiting this center to write valentines to their classmates and then deposit them in the mailbox. At the end of center time, empty the mailbox and deliver the hearty greetings!

Heart Art

Children will be delighted to make these fancy hearts all by themselves! In advance, collect different sizes of empty thread spools. For each child, duplicate the heart pattern (page 39) on red or pink construction paper. Arrange the heart patterns and spools in a center along with white tempera paint, paintbrushes, and slightly damp sponges. Provide sheets of red, pink, or white construction paper; scissors; and glue for the backing. Instruct a child to paint a thin coat of white paint onto a sponge. Then have her use the painted sponge as a stamp pad, pressing one end of a spool into the sponge and then onto the heart cutout as desired. When the paint is dry, have each child cut out her heart and then mount it on a sheet of construction paper.

Once Upon a Fairy Tale

Reinforce skills across the curriculum in true fairy-tale fashion!

by Mackie Rhodes

I Can Tell the Story!

Develop story comprehension and vocabulary with this unique twist on story retelling! In advance, share your favorite versions of *The Three Little Pigs, Goldilocks and the Three Bears,* and *The Three Billy Goats Gruff.* Then arrange the books in a center along with some story-related props, such as a brick and a bundle of sticks to represent the tale of the pigs, a bowl and a toy chair for the story of the bears, and a toy bridge and green Easter grass for the goats' story. Instruct children to visit this center in groups of two or three. Have each child select a prop and find the story to which it relates. Then ask each child to use the props and the pictures in the books and tell what happened in the story that relates to that prop. Hey, I can tell about that!

Familiar Faces

Here's a fun art activity that brings your students face-to-face with their favorite fairy-tale characters. Stock your art center with drawing paper, scissors, glue, crayons or markers, and a photo of each child. For this activity, have a child cut out her face from her photo and mount it on a sheet of paper. Then encourage her to draw a fairy-tale character using her face as the face of the character. Finally, have her write or dictate about her illustration. Gee, you look so familiar!

Size 'em Up

Straightening up after those well-known three bears builds size discrimination and sorting skills. To prepare this center, enlarge, photocopy and laminate the size labels on page 43. Collect groups of items in small, medium, and large sizes, such as bowls, plates, spoons, shoes, and teddy bears. Place all the items in a laundry basket; then put the laundry basket and the size labels in your math center. When a child visits this center, have him lay out the size labels. Then ask him to find all of the items belonging to one set, such as all the bowls. Next, have him sort that set according to the size labels. Is it small, medium, or large?

Math Center

sorting ◄
size discrimination ◄
vocabulary ◄

*Ting Tang Ting Tang
Ting Tang Ting Tang*

Blocks Center

exploration ◄
sound discrimination ◄
listening skills ◄

Trip, Trap, Trip, Trap!

What sounds do you think you'd hear if the billy goats Gruff came walking across a bridge near you? Invite youngsters to explore this question with hands-on discovery. Stock your blocks center with a collection of different bridge-building materials, such as wooden blocks, plastic containers, metal baking pans, and corrugated cardboard. Also add a few sets of rhythm sticks. Then encourage students to use the supplies to build bridges. When the bridges are constructed, instruct children to use the rhythm sticks to resemble goats' hooves walking across the bridges. Here they come! What do you hear?

Yes	No	Yes	No	Yes	No
Straw		Sticks		Brick	

Discovery Center

▶ observation skills
▶ experimentation

Huffin' and Puffin'

Could that big bad wolf *really* have blown a house down? Invite your students to do some investigating to come up with their own responses to that question. To prepare, arrange the house-building materials from *The Three Little Pigs*—some straw (or raffia), some small sticks, and a brick. For this activity, have a child blow through a clean drinking straw to try to move the house-building supplies. Then invite him to record his conclusions about the wolf's success on a graph similar to the one shown. During a group time, discuss what the graph reveals. What's the consensus?

Dramatic-Play Center

▶ role-playing
▶ creative thinking
▶ verbal language

Places, Everyone!

All creative thinking caps must be securely fastened for this ad-libbing activity! In advance, duplicate the role-playing cards (page 43) on construction paper. Color and cut apart the cards; then laminate them. Place the cards facedown in your dramatic-play area. Provide a variety of fairy-tale props that correspond with the characters on the cards. When you open this center, instruct children to visit the area in groups of two or more. Have each child draw a card to determine what her part will be. When each child has a role, let the playing begin!

Size Labels
Use with "Size 'em Up" on page 41.
Role-Playing Cards
Use with "Places, Everyone!" on page 42.

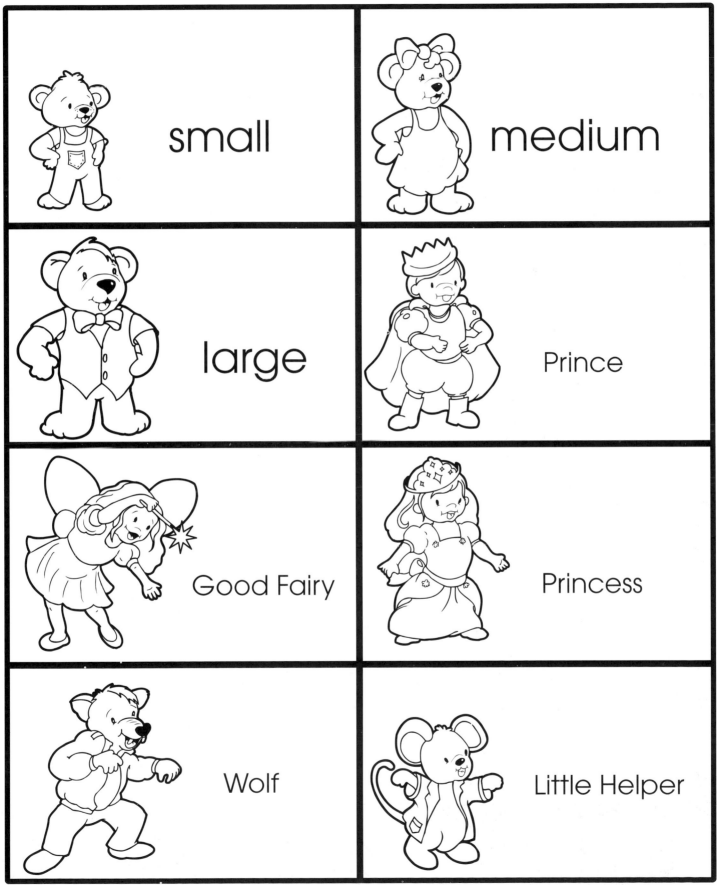

small

medium

large

Prince

Good Fairy

Princess

Wolf

Little Helper

43

It's Nursery Rhyme Time!

Your little ones are headed for a treasury of cross-curricular learning fun when they visit these centers highlighting some of their favorite rhymes.

by Suzanne Moore

Jumping Jacks and Jills!

Just how nimble and quick are your students? Find out with a roll of the die! To make a die, cover a cube-shaped tissue box with colorful paper or an adhesive covering. Use sticky dots or a permanent marker to program the dots on the die. Place the die in the center along with six large laminated candle cutouts. When a child visits this center, instruct her to arrange the candles each about two feet apart in a row. Then have her roll the die, count the dots, and jump over that many candles (one at a time). For an added challenge, have the child roll the die, count the dots, and arrange that many candles side by side. Then have her try to jump over the group of candles all at once! Jack and Jill be nimble!

Math Center

▶ counting
▶ spatial awareness
▶ gross-motor skills

Rub-a-dub-dub

Rub-a-dub-dub, how many in a tub? That's what your classroom crew will find out when they make active learning discoveries at this water-filled table. First, gather a supply of small waterproof toy people and animal figures and a variety of empty food tubs. Arrange the supplies near your water table. When youngsters visit this center, encourage them to fill the tubs with varying numbers of toy people and animals. How many people fit inside any given tub before it starts to tip? Will the tub sink completely? Does each tub hold the same number of people? It's rub-a-dub-dub discovery fun!

Sensory Center

▶ experimentation
▶ observation
▶ analytical thinking

Discovery Center

observation skills ◄
experimentation ◄
making comparisons ◄

Down the Hill!

Oops! Jack and Jill *tumbled* down the hill, but your youngsters will make lots of discoveries as they help toy cars *roll* down this hill. To prepare, create a ramp (hill) by placing a smooth piece of wood on a stack of blocks from your block center. When a child visits this center, have her position a toy car at the top of the ramp and then let go and watch it roll down. How far did the car roll? Encourage the child to change the height of the ramp and then repeat the roll. Did the car roll further when the ramp was higher or lower? How about another car? Same or different results?

London Bridges

Youngsters cruise into creativity as they construct numerous bridges and then *help* the bridges fall! In advance, cut a length of blue bulletin board paper to resemble a river; then tape it to the floor in your block area. When children visit this center, encourage them to sing a few rounds of "London Bridge" as they cooperatively build and rebuild bridges across the river. Get ready! London Bridge is about to fall down!

Block Center

problem solving ◄
creative thinking ◄
spatial awareness ◄

Mark It With a B!

Students bake up a big batch of language skills when they create these special letter cakes. In advance, stock the center with play dough, a rolling pin, plastic knives, spatulas, foam trays (to use as cookie sheets), and a shoebox (to use as an oven). Write the "Pat-a-Cake" nursery rhyme on chart paper; then display it in the center. Encourage each baker to read/recite the rhyme as he rolls out the dough. Then have him cut out a cake. Next, have him use the knife to mark it with a *B* and then slide it onto a tray and into the oven. To extend this activity, encourage each child to create a cake for each letter of his name. Bake me some letter cakes as fast as you can!

Literacy Center

▶ *oral language*
▶ *experience with print*
▶ *writing skills*

Pat-a-Cake
Pat-a-cake, pat-a-cake, baker's man.
Bake me a cake as fast as you can.
Roll it, and pat it, and mark it with a *B*.
Then put it in the oven for baby and me!

Mary's Sure-to-Go Snacks

Your students will flock to this center to make these tempting snacks. In advance, copy, color, and cut out the recipe cards on page 47. Display the cards in sequence in your cooking area. When a child visits this center, invite him to follow the directions to make a snack for himself. This great snack is sure to go with each of your little lambs!

Cooking Center

▶ *eye-hand coordination*
▶ *measurement*
▶ *following directions*

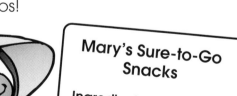

Mary's Sure-to-Go Snacks

Ingredients for each child:
¼ c. mini pretzel twists
yogurt-covered raisins
O-shaped cereal
M&M's® candies

Utensils and supplies:
one zippered plastic bag per child
¼ c. measuring cup
1 tbsp. measuring spoon

Teacher preparation:
Arrange the ingredients and supplies for easy student access.

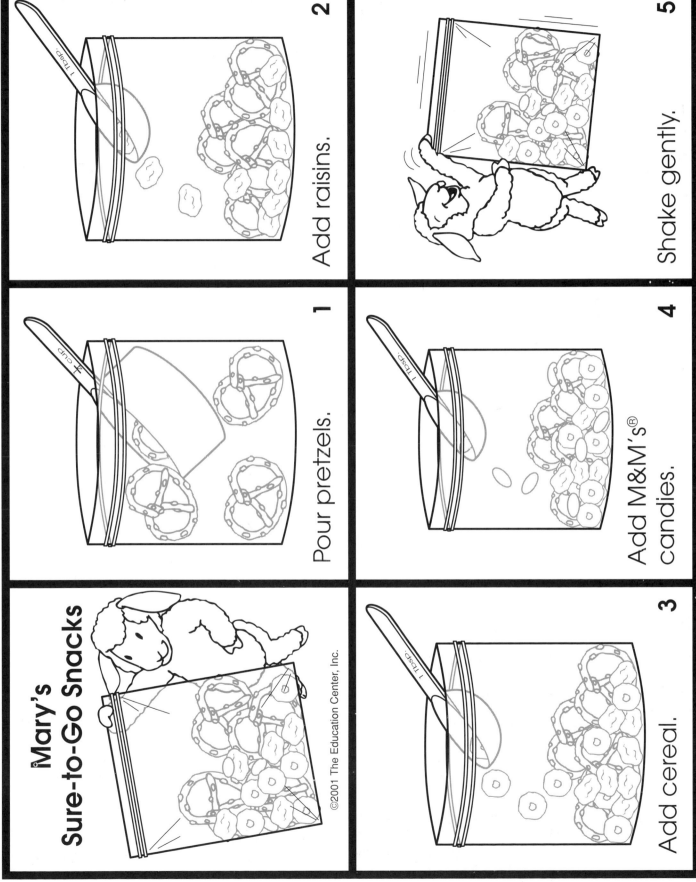

2 Add raisins.

5 Shake gently.

1 Pour pretzels.

4 Add M&M's® candies.

Mary's Sure-to-Go Snacks

©2001 The Education Center, Inc.

3 Add cereal.

Construction Zone

Set up these construction centers and watch little ones build their skills in a variety of curriculum areas.

by Mackie Rhodes

Literacy Center

▶ vocabulary
▶ letter recognition
▶ word recognition

Word Wall

Build a firm foundation of literacy skills with this interactive wallpaper! In advance, "wallpaper" your literacy center walls with home improvement ads. Also, fill the pockets of a carpenter's apron with magnetic letters. When a child visits this center, have her remove a letter from one of the pockets. Next, ask her to search the wallpaper to find words (or pictures of things) beginning with that letter. Have her use a highlighter to circle the words or pictures. For younger children, have them just identify and highlight the corresponding letters found in the ads. Literacy is going up, up, up!

Math Center

▶ estimation skills
▶ counting
▶ making comparisons

Nuts and Bolts

Get down to the nuts and bolts of estimating at this math center. To prepare, collect a supply of large nut-and-bolt sets. Separate the nuts and bolts into two different bowls. Arrange the bowls in a center along with two clear plastic jars and writing utensils. Invite students to visit this center in pairs. Ask one child to put a random number of nuts in one jar while the other child puts a random number of bolts in the other jar. Then have each child look at the jar he did not fill and guess how many items are in that jar. Have him write down his guess and then count to find out the actual total. Was the actual number more than, less than, or equal to his guess?

Hard Hat Hide-and-Seek

There's a very special attraction in this science center! In advance, collect three plastic hard hats (without the inside padding and straps) and an assortment of metal hardware items, such as hinges and large washers. Set these items in a center along with a roll of masking tape and a strong bar magnet. Invite children to visit this center in pairs. To do this activity, instruct one child to tape a piece of hardware inside the top of one of the hats. Then have him mix up the hats and arrange them in a row. Next, ask his partner to guess which hat contains the hardware. Have the partner use the magnet to check her guess. What an exciting discovery when one of the hats responds to the magnet by moving! Have the partners switch roles and repeat the activity as often as desired. It's magnetic!

Discovery Center

problem solving ◀
observation ◀
experimenting ◀

Construction Crunchies

These creative snacks build imaginations! Stock your cooking center with a supply of pretzel sticks and assorted shapes and sizes of crackers. Add a container of cream cheese spread or peanut butter along with a class supply of plastic knives, paper plates, and napkins. Then invite each child to construct a cracker-and-pretzel creation using the cream cheese or peanut butter to cement his structure together. When each child's creation has been viewed, munch and crunch away! Little ones will definitely enjoy this edible architecture!

Cooking Center

fine-motor skills ◀
creative ◀
expression
spatial ◀
relationships

▶ *listening skills*
▶ *creative thinking*
▶ *rhythm*

Toolbox Tunes

Invite your little workers to create their own musical masterpieces with some simple tools of the trade. To prepare, stock a toolbox with items such as wrenches, small blocks of wood, PVC pipes, nuts and bolts, and any other tools with unique, noise-producing potential. Put the toolbox, a few hard hats, and a recording of upbeat music in a center. Then invite a child to turn on the music and use the tools, hard hats, and even the toolbox to gently experiment with sounds and rhythm. Now that's constructive instrumentation!

Metal Search

Here's a sensory center that's sure to attract attention! Bury small metal nuts, bolts, and washers in a tub of cedar shavings (available at pet supply stores). Encourage little ones to use magnets to collect the metal items from among the cedar shavings. Then have them assemble the nut, bolt, and washer sets. How many sets did you find?

▶ *visual
  discrimination*
▶ *fine-motor skills*
▶ *tactile experience*

Textured Blueprints

Students design their own original blueprints with this unique idea! For each child, cut off the edges of a foam tray so that a flat sheet of foam remains. Put the adapted trays in your art center along with a shallow container of blue tempera paint mixed with a few drops of liquid soap. To make a blueprint design, instruct a child to use a dull pencil to draw a house or building on one side of the tray. Then have her use a small roller or paintbrush to apply paint to the design. Next, have her press the painted surface onto a sheet of paper. Finally, instruct her to carefully remove the tray to reveal a blueprint of her picture. When the paint is dry, display all the works of art on a bulletin board. Great design!

Art Center

fine-motor skills ◀
creative ◀
expression
spatial awareness ◀

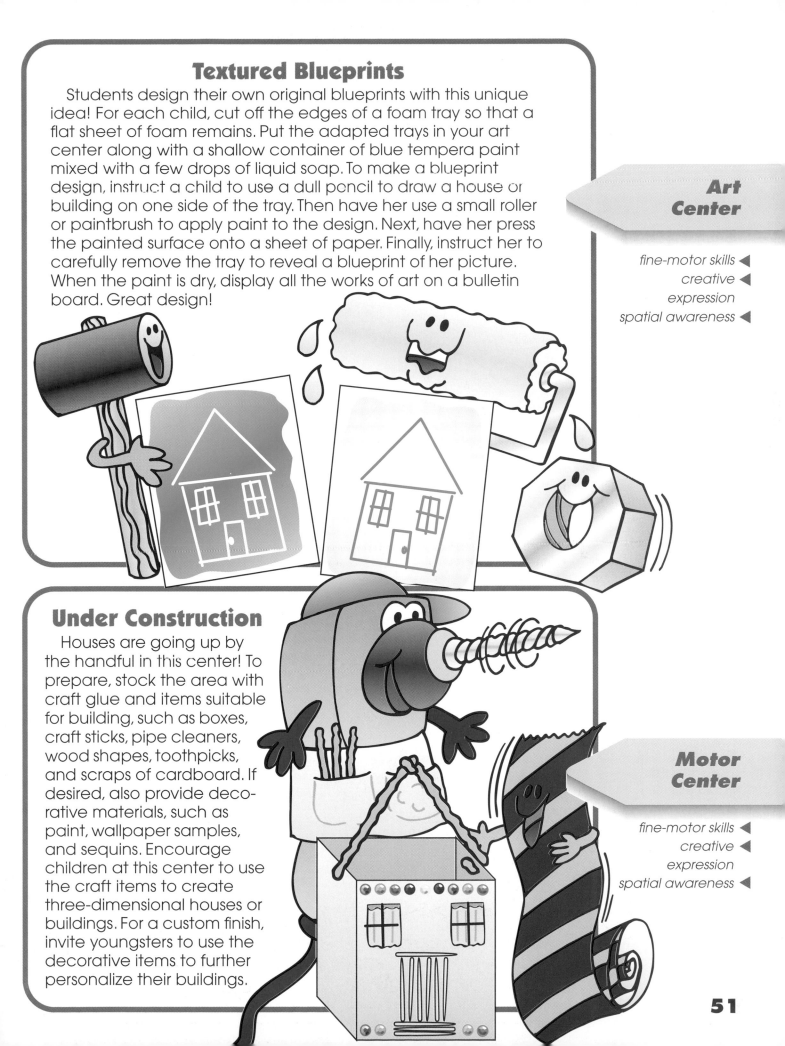

Under Construction

Houses are going up by the handful in this center! To prepare, stock the area with craft glue and items suitable for building, such as boxes, craft sticks, pipe cleaners, wood shapes, toothpicks, and scraps of cardboard. If desired, also provide decorative materials, such as paint, wallpaper samples, and sequins. Encourage children at this center to use the craft items to create three-dimensional houses or buildings. For a custom finish, invite youngsters to use the decorative items to further personalize their buildings.

Motor Center

fine-motor skills ◀
creative ◀
expression
spatial awareness ◀

African Traditions

Provide lots of active learning with classroom centers that highlight African traditions.

by Missy Hauck

Literacy Center

▶ creative writing
▶ oral language
▶ fine-motor skills

A Long Time Ago...

In many African villages, wonderful storytelling revolves around animals and people that lived long ago. At this center, your youngsters become the storytellers! To prepare, provide a variety of pictures of African animals and people. Place them in your center along with a supply of paper and crayons. For inspiration, invite a child to look through the pictures. Then encourage him to write and illustrate a story about animals or people that lived long ago in Africa. During a group time, have each child share his story with the class.

Suggested Literature
(all authored by Ifeoma Onyefulu)
A Is for Africa
Chidi Only Likes Blue: An African Book of Colors
Emeka's Gift: An African Counting Story

The lion ran into the jungle!

Sensory Center

▶ tactile experience
▶ fine-motor skills
▶ creative expression

Sand Drawings

Some African children like to draw pictures in the sand around their houses. Your students will be able to do the same thing with this tactile drawing activity! Pour a layer of sand into a sensory tub; then add some clean pebbles and sticks. Invite children to use their fingers, the sticks, and the pebbles to create simple pictures in the sand. As they do, they'll be sharing a common experience with children in Africa. Pictures really are universal!

Steady Now!

Have you ever tried to balance something on your head? Some women in Africa can carry a basket or jug on their heads while they're walking! Get ready for lots of giggles when your youngsters try to master this African custom. In advance, transform your dramatic-play area into an African market by stocking it with plastic bowls, plates, and play food. As each child visits this center, encourage him to fill a bowl or plate with food and then balance the bowl on his head as he tries to walk from one side of the market to the other. No doubt youngsters will gain a real appreciation for this method of transporting goods!

Dramatic-Play Center

gross-motor skills ◄
role-playing ◄
cultural awareness ◄

Clay Pots

In many African countries, earthenware pots are used to store water. Get ready for a burst of creativity when your students create their own clay pots. Set up a center with a supply of self-drying clay. Encourage each child to mold her clay into any type of pot. Demonstrate how to add details by adding small clay ropes or balls of clay. With adult supervision, instruct each child to straighten out one end of a paper clip. Then have her use the straight end to scratch designs in her pot. Set the finished projects in a warm, dry area until they are dry (two to three days).

Art Center

creative expression ◄
fine-motor skills ◄
tactile experience ◄

Music and
Movement
Center

▶ listening skills
▶ reproducing
  rhythms
▶ gross-motor skills

Pa-Rum Pum Pum Pum

Not only are African drums used to make music, but they are also used as a way to announce special meetings or important news to the community. In advance, collect several different types of hand drums. Before opening the center, demonstrate appropriate uses of the instruments. Then invite children to visit the center in small groups. Encourage children to explore the drums. How many different sounds can be made with each drum? What happens if they strike the drums with different parts of their hands? Have one child drum a rhythm. Can another child repeat it? What drumming fun!

Math
Center

▶ patterning
▶ fine-motor skills
▶ spatial
  relationships

Stripes!

What animal has black and white stripes all over? A zebra, of course! And this interesting African animal provides just the opportunity to practice patterning skills! To prepare, copy the zebra pattern (page 55) onto white construction paper to create a class supply. Place the patterns in your center along with a supply of black crayons. Then invite each child to color the zebra so that it shows a black and white repeating pattern. Did you know that no two zebras' stripes are exactly alike?

100th Day Celebration!

Add these activities to your centers to join in one of the most anticipated and celebrated days for little learners!

by Roxanne LaBell Dearman

Math Center

▶ *estimation*
▶ *recording information*
▶ *counting*

I Spy 100!

Can your students spy 100? Find out when they visit this math center. To prepare, program a sheet of chart paper similar to the one shown. Gather three clear plastic jars. Fill one jar with exactly 100 small items, such as buttons, small candies, or dried beans. Fill the second jar with *more* than 100 of a different item, and a third jar with *less* than 100 of a third item. Secure the lid on each jar; then attach a different-colored sticky note to the top of each lid. Also provide a supply of sticky notes in each color. Guide each center visitor to examine the jars. Invite him to guess which jar has exactly 100 things in it. Have him record his guess by writing his initials on the corresponding color of sticky note and then attaching it in the appropriate place on the graph. During a group time, discuss what the graph reveals. Then chorally count the contents of each jar until you find the one with 100!

Which Jar Has 100?

AB	JA	
RS	TJ	MT
GW	LJ	CO
	RN	DE
	GF	WA
	JC	HI
	DE	

Sensory Center

▶ *tactile experience*
▶ *fine-motor skills*
▶ *counting*

The Hidden Hundred

Do you have 100 marbles? Beads? Pennies? Great! Add them to your sand table along with slotted spoons, funnels, and sifters. Invite small groups of children to work together to find all 100 items. To help them keep track of counting, encourage children to arrange their findings in rows or stacks of ten. When the children have ten rows or stacks, help them count by tens to 100. Oh, my! That's 100!

100th Day Posters

There's a whole lot of stamping going on in this art center! Stock your art area with a class supply of large sheets of light-colored construction paper. Also provide a variety of rubber stamps and colorful stamp pads. To create a poster, instruct a child to make ten rows with ten stamps in each row. For example, one child might choose to stamp 100 hearts, while another child opts to stamp ten rows of ten different stamps. After each child shares his poster, count together by tens until you reach the end of the poster and 100. Then display the posters for independent counting practice.

Art Center

creative expression ◄
spatial awareness ◄
counting ◄

Spending Hundreds

Strengthen writing skills with this pretend check-writing activity! Tell students that in honor of 100th Day, the snack for the day will cost each child $100! (If desired, use the cooking idea on page 58.) And since nobody carries around that much cash—especially in preschool and kindergarten—everybody will need to write a check! To prepare, use the check patterns on page 59 to make a few more than a class supply of checks. Place the checks in your writing center along with a supply of writing utensils. (If desired, fill out one of the check patterns to use as a sample.) When a child visits this center, encourage her to fill in the check and then sign her name at the bottom of it. My, how grown-up you are!

Literacy Center

left-to-right ◄
progression
experience with print ◄
writing skills ◄

Just "Dough" It

Roll and shape some fine-motor fun into your 100th Day celebrations! Stock a center with a batch of your favorite play dough. (If desired, add a festive touch to the play dough by kneading in some colorful confetti.) Also provide rolling pins and craft sticks. When a child visits this center, encourage her to shape the play dough into the number 100. Or have her use a craft stick to "write" the number 100 in rolled-out play dough. This fine-motor practice is "dough-lightful"!

100 Snack

Looking for a simple snack that your little ones can prepare independently? Try this neat treat in your cooking center! In preparation, gather ten bowls. Fill each bowl with a different snack item, such as raisins, mini marshmallows, chocolate chips, and cereal pieces. Place the filled bowls in your center along with a tray, a supply of portion cups, and a resealable plastic bag for each child. To make a snack, a child arranges ten portion cups on the tray. Next, he takes ten items from the first bowl and puts them in his first portion cup. He continues in this manner for each of the ten bowls. Finally, he pours each cup's contents into the plastic bag. Wow! That's 100!

School Bank

Date _____

Pay to the
Order of _____ $ [   ]

_____

_____
Name

ABC☆123☆ABC☆123

©2001 The Education Center, Inc.

School Bank

Date _____

Pay to the
Order of _____ $ [   ]

_____

_____
Name

ABC☆123☆ABC☆123

©2001 The Education Center, Inc.

Bedtime!

Snuggle up to lots of cuddly, cozy learning with these bedtime centers!

by Suzanne Moore

Literacy Center

- visual discrimination
- experience with print
- vocabulary

Nighty-Night Lotto

Little ones will love this lively lotto game featuring familiar bedtime pictures. To prepare this game, make two copies each of pages 63–64 on white construction paper. Color each page so that the matching pictures look the same. Laminate the pages; then make playing cards by cutting apart the squares of only one copy of each page. Place the deck of cards facedown in your center along with the lotto boards. To play, a child takes a card from the stack. If she has a matching picture on her selected lotto board, she places the card on top of it. If she does not have a matching picture, she returns her card to the bottom of the pile. She continues play in this manner until she has matched all of her cards to the pictures on her board. (This game can be played with one or two players.)

Motor Center

- fine-motor skills
- gross-motor skills
- problem solving

Linens and Such

Visiting this center is sure to be heaps of fun for little hands. In advance, stock a couple of laundry baskets with various sizes of pillows, pillowcases, and small sheets. Put the baskets in a center. Then invite youngsters to practice putting the pillows inside the pillowcases and folding the sheets. And if a little teamwork shows up in this center, all the better!

Splish, Splash!

Before bedtime comes a bath, of course! So get your classroom crew ready for some bubbly fun! Pour children's bubble bath into a tub of water and then swish it around to create bubbles. Add a few bath toys to the water along with a couple of washcloths. Also provide towels for drying both the toys and children's hands. Then let bath time begin for lots of squeaky-clean learning play!

Sensory Center

fine-motor skills ◄
sensory ◄
experience
socialization ◄

Blanket and Pillow Match

Tuck in math skills with this blanket and pillow matching activity. For each number that you'd like to include in this activity, cut out two felt rectangles to resemble pillows. Program one pillow with a number and the other with a corresponding set of sticky dots. Next, program half sheets of light-colored construction paper (blankets) with matching number words; then laminate them. Use a shoebox lid to resemble a bed and place the blanket on top of it. (Trim the blanket to fit if necessary.) When a child visits this center, have him "make" each bed by matching a numbered pillow to its corresponding pillow and blanket. For easy self-checking, just program the backs of each matching blanket and pillow set with corresponding colors or shapes. No snoring here—just lots of cozy matching!

Math Center

number ◄
recognition
number word ◄
recognition
counting ◄

It's Brushing Time!

A good toothbrushing is *always* in order before bedtime! Give little ones some realistic practice removing stains with a toothbrush at this hands-on center. In advance, use grape juice or strong tea to stain several hard-boiled eggs or white ceramic tiles (available at home improvement stores). Stock your center with toothbrushes, toothpaste, and a container of water. Also add a roll of paper towels for quick clean-ups. When a child visits this center, have her squirt an appropriate amount of toothpaste onto a toothbrush and then brush the stained object sparkly clean.

Time for Bed

Feeling sleepy? It must be time for bed! Create a cozy bedtime corner in your dramatic-play area. Arrange a few pillows and blankets in the area; then add some adult robes and fuzzy slippers. If desired, also add a few stuffed animals and rocking chairs, too. Of course, little ones will want to hear a bedtime story before going to sleep, so be sure to keep favorite books available nearby. Invite youngsters to visit the center, don the bedtime attire, and take a little rest—real or pretend. Or perhaps they'd like to pretend to be a family nearing bedtime. What a cozy little corner!

Nighty-Night Lotto

yawn

toothbrush

pajamas

water

bed

slippers

Nighty-Night Lotto

quilt

bathtub

stuffed animal

book

pillow

night-light